CAT BLESSINGS

by Bob Lovka

illustrations by Setsu Broderick

A COLLECTION OF
POEMS, QUOTES,
FACTS, & MYTHS

BOWTIE™
P R E S S

IRVINE, CALIFORNIA

Amy Fox, editor
Nick Clemente, special consultant
Book design and layout by Michele Lanci-Altomare

The cats in this book are alternately referred to as *he* and *she* throughout the book.

Library of Congress Control Number: 2001095701

BowTie™ Press
A Division of Fancy Publications
3 Burroughs
Irvine, California 92618
(949) 855-8822

Printed and Bound in Singapore
10 9 8 7 6 5 4 3 2 1

DEDICATION

To Marge Weems, founder and director of Angel Puss Rescue in California's San Fernando Valley, whose boundless love and tireless dedication to weak, helpless, and homeless feral cats is a blessing fit for any angel. —B.L.

For Kyle, Raulie, Jenna, Parker, and Wyatt. —S.B.

INTRODUCTION

Cats are heaven-sent blessings, coming to us as a complex species living *in* our human world but living *of* a world that is totally their own. Cats are part of the little magical mysteries of life: much the way a flower grows or the wind invisibly moves through the trees. Cats remind us that there's more to our existence than meets the eye.

Cats also bring personal blessings such as companionship, joy, and comfort to us. Petting a purring cat can lower our blood pressure a bit;

mimicking a cat's luxurious stretch is a good exercise for keeping ourselves loose and limber; and hygienically, who's cleaner than the cat? (Okay, maybe a goldfish, but trying to pet one will raise the blood pressure, not lower it.)

Cats, and the way they bless our lives, touch something within us. Watch a cat watching you, and you'll find a deep communication in the feline gaze. Watch a cat as she "meditates," staring out toward…what?…and you'll find yourself looking at the invisible only a cat can see. In quiet moments, a cat can take you outside yourself.

Cats have been regarded as mystical and mysterious, honored as angelic, and reviled as evil emissaries. The multifaceted cat continues to fascinate us. Cats seem "to know something," but they're not telling.

This splendid little book is a celebration of the cats who occupy the world with us. Author Jules Verne wrote, "I believe cats to be spirits come to earth. A cat, I am sure, could walk on a cloud without coming through." May we always be open to the little blessings and special wonders they bring.

The Character of a Cat

Patient
Discreet
With no tales to tell.
And as for keeping secrets
Few do it as well.

A carriage of Grace
An air of Dignity
Assured and Proud, yet Playful
A thinker Independently.

Such are the qualities
found in a cat.
Who among humans
can claim all of that?

KITTY &
MORRIS
FAMILY

A CAT'S WHISKERS

Whiskers are not a fashion statement or an endorsement for facial hair (so please don't ever trim or wash them!). A cat's whiskers are very sensitive and give a cat an incredible amount of "radar."

Whiskers tell a cat:

the parameter of space she's entering

air movements and pressure

the shape and movement of her prey

When the cat's whiskers droop, rain is near.

—ENGLISH FOLKLORE

A cat uses whiskers to measure air movement and pressure. Whiskers tell a cat the parameters of any space she's entering and signal whether she'll fit into, under, or next to an object. A cat even uses whiskers when hunting to zero in on the shape of the prey and determine how the prey is moving.

As air moves around objects, cat whiskers vibrate and pick up signals. (Gillette and Schick would be out of business if human whiskers could do that!) Whiskers help a cat identify her surroundings, letting her move through her world with confidence. And they allow her to sense the size and shape of obstacles and spaces without having to see them or touch them first. Whiskers are a big reason why cats are able to maneuver so well in the dark, rarely stubbing their toes on the way to the bathroom as we do.

There are about twelve movable whiskers on each side of a cat's nose, and they're more than twice as thick as a human hair. They're arranged in rows, and the bottom two rows can move independently of the top two. The most mischievous of cats will quickly wiggle their whiskers then stop and walk away just as you stare and try to confirm what you think you saw is really what you saw. It's all part of the behavior known as The Fun of Unnerving Humans. Whiskers also help cats detect odors—so if you see the cat's whiskers twitching and the cat run off as you approach, it may be time for a bath.

When the cat's whiskers droop, the cat's face is wet! —FLUFFY

Of Most Special Interest

Mice scampering along the baseboards
Flutter-wings of darting birds
Tiny holes and cracks and crevices
Crawling, running spiders and bugs
Opened bags
and almost closed doors.

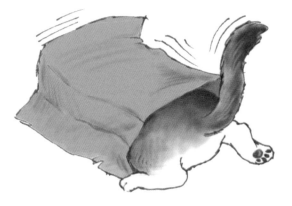

The Composite Cat

Intelligent and Discerning,

Affectionate in her own terms.

Studious and Curious

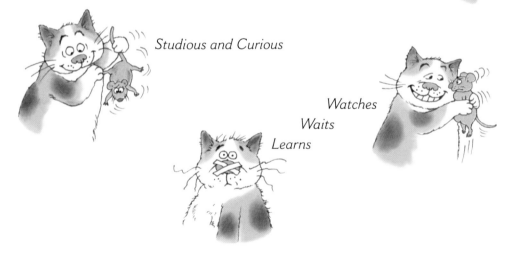

Watches

Waits

Learns

In Lewis Carroll's *Through the Looking Glass,* Alice thinks it most inconvenient that kittens purr in response to whatever one might say to them. She wished that cats would set up some system of distinctive speech, such as a meow for no and a purr for yes rather than using—at least to her ear—the same sound for any conversation. Cat lovers outside of the

looking glass, however, know that cats do have a definite vocabulary and that their conversations with us can be quite a blessing.

Cats communicate both nonverbally, through body language and scent, and verbally, through sounds. This inherited behavior expresses their emotions, attitudes, and intentions. Humans might not understand all the nuances of a stare, a movement shift, or the difference between a low-pitched and high-pitched yowl, but the feline recipient of such communiqués reads them like a book, explaining what's going on in the other cat's mind.

On the sound front, cats produce vocal sounds such as meows, growls, and throaty gurgles from the voice box, but they can also generate nonvocal sounds such as purring, hissing, and quivering, which don't come from the voice box. Cats are ventriloquists, throwing sounds around! Scientific studies have found more than a dozen distinctive sound utterings, but cats are likely to discern many others. Mix, match, and combine them, and it adds up to a cat alphabet that describes their world.

My cat, Sonny, is a great communicator. His sphinxlike stance and regal stare from atop the kitchen table late at night signals me that it's time for a snack or treat. When I respond with an acknowledging, "What?" Sonny comes back with a quick, definite meow (translation: "What do you think?!") and continues to fix me with "the stare" until the request is met.

He also sprints to the front door and offers a high-pitched mew for "Outside."
He prances and gives a more plaintive mew at the back door if the demand at the front door doesn't work.

Cats are blessed with knowing how to make us understand what they want without actually telling us. They take the initiative in their interactions with us, blessing us with a genuinely dynamic, two-sided relationship. Communicating across the species boundary puts us in touch with something beyond the physically defined plain on which we live. We're blessed to have a glimpse of something beyond.

Cats were originally created with wings to allow them mobility to roam; but being great hunters the cats used their wings to prey on birds. Seeing the birds face extinction, God took away the cats' wings and turned their flutter into a purr.

—EASTERN EUROPEAN FOLKLORE

From the Cat's Mouth

In speaking to you,
I'll never shout
For I expect you to know
What I'm talking about!

There's my stare that means one thing
And my me-yoww that means another
And if I say rowwl, it's frustration,
Like saying, Oh, Brother!

There's a sound for "Outdoors"
And the call for a meal.
If you're petting too much
I might even squeal.

My vocabulary is rich
And not so difficult to discern.
Just pay attention:
Watch and listen—you'll learn!

OVERLOOKED AND MISUNDERSTOOD FELINE BLESSINGS, AND WHAT THEY TEACH US:

FROM A CAT'S CONSTANT CLEANING AND PREENING: A sense of fastidiousness.

BY NOT COMING WHEN CALLED: An appreciation of the true spirit of independence.

THROUGH SLEEPING SIXTEEN HOURS A DAY AND NAPPING FREQUENTLY IN BETWEEN: A reminder of the power of relaxation.

FROM LIMITLESS CURIOSITY: An affirmation of the wonders inherent in the little matters at hand.

BY VIRTUE OF SHREDDING UPHOLSTERY AND TATTERING DRAPES: An acute awareness of climb over matter.

Feline Forever Young

Facials?
Spas?
Mud packs, perhaps,
Just to preserve fleeting youth?

No way!
Uh-Uh!
A feline makeover
Sounds so uncouth!

For in spite of birthdays,
A cat's beauty stays.
Eyes bright with a deep, piercing stare.
And as for the face
There's nary a trace
That a wrinkle appears anywhere.

Living with Cats

Companions in fur coats
doing as they wish.
One moment they're cute and lovely
the next, aloof and snobbish.

When you want play,
they have other things to do.
For playtime, you see,
is not up to you.

A cat will watch you
Stare at you
Causing you to wonder what she knows

You can take nothing for granted.
Cats keep you on your toes.

THE ANALYTICAL CAT

Blessed with analytical (and curious) minds, cats look before leaping.

Headstrong in will but sensibly cautious in action, cats approach the new or unusual with a seeming logic rather than emotion.

First, there's a visual reconnaissance and a check of the mental banks to determine if the new object or situation resembles something previously encountered. Then, there's a sniff of the air for olfactory signals of anything familiar. A cautious, measured advance is next to see if movement and approach elicit any new information from the mysterious element ahead. Finally, there's a close inspection for further identification, and then tactile contact, as if to say, *Let's see what this feels like.*

A cat's a cat and that's that.

—AMERICAN FOLK SAYING

A cat studies the newfound, registers it into the labyrinth of his cat mind, then, having conquered the "new" world, calmly walks away. Not a bad lesson for the two-legged among us.

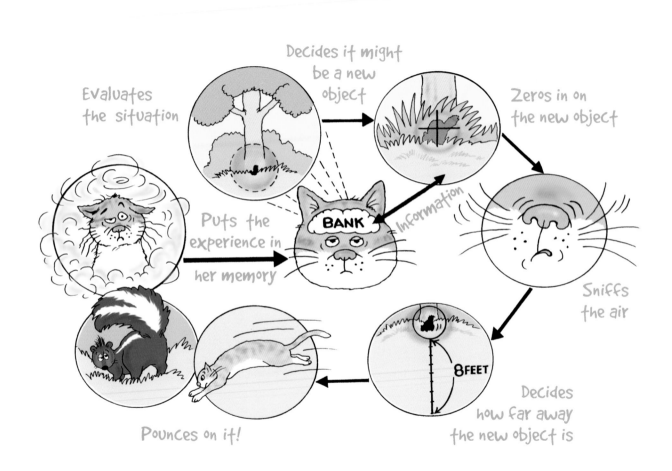

Evaluates the situation

Decides it might be a new object

Zeros in on the new object

Puts the experience in her memory

BANK

Information

Sniffs the air

Pounces on it!

8 FEET

Decides how far away the new object is

A cat's brain more closely resembles a human's than it does a dog's brain. Ask any cat and he'll be thrilled to point that out. Cats and humans have identical regions in their brains that are responsible for emotion. Yet, humans often use their brains to approach the new with the emotion of fear. Encountering the "new" brings change, and change is inevitable, so we'd better adapt somehow! Cats may offer a clue: approach the new with curiosity rather than fear or a heady rush into who knows what. Be open to change and seek out any familiarity; everything has some link to something we already know. Weigh the risks, then go forward and meet the challenge if warranted. Once you do, you'll find that the new isn't so scary after all, and in fact, it might just be a better version of the same old thing. Take the blessed approach of a brainy cool cat rather than an emotional 'fraidy cat.

BLESSED RELIGIOUSLY, MYTHICALLY, AND SYMBOLICALLY

Throughout world history—biblical times, ancient Egypt, the Roman Empire, medieval times—cats have left their pawprints upon our material and spiritual worlds and continue to do so today.

Although the Bible makes no specific mention of the cat—possibly because cats were being worshiped as pagan gods in Egypt at the time the Bible was being written—there is a legend that on Noah's ark the mouse and rat populations were taking the order to "go forth and multiply" much too seriously and were causing havoc on the ark. Responding to Noah's prayer, God caused the resident lions to sneeze and out came the cat. Score one for a blessing of pest control!

The Koran, the Islamic book of sacred writings, actually cautions us to treat cats favorably. The Koran mentions a woman who was tortured and put in hell because she kept a cat locked up until he died of hunger, giving us a reminder that we should bless cats with kindness in return for their blessings to us.

The prophet Muhammad shared his life with a cat named Meuzza, who was a model for teaching the great prophet patience. It is said that the cat once fell asleep on

Muhammad's arm, curled into his robe. Rather than wake his companion, Muhammad cut the sleeve from the robe when he wished to leave and left the dozing cat undisturbed. A blessed sleep for the cat and a lot of patience displayed by Muhammad, indeed!

The prophet enjoyed the company of cats, and according to the Koran, forbade selling a cat for money or traded goods. It is written that there is no harm in allowing a cat to drink from your bowl since it is believed that there are no impurities in the cat's saliva unless there are visible impurities on the cat's mouth. Not much chance of that with cats being as hygienic as they are!

Around the fifth century A.D. Chinese and Japanese mystics believed that good people were reincarnated as cats, not as humans. Some Buddhist and Hindu sects believe that on the reincarnation path, going to a cat life from a human one is a step up the ladder toward the perfect state of nirvana. So much for leading a dog's life.

As for being directly blessed, cats are connected to many ancient deities. Diana and Artemis were both considered the mother of cats. Diana's hunting prowess reflects the hunting ability of cats. The Roman goddess, Liberty, is usually portrayed with a cat at her feet, and the Egyptian fertility goddess, Bastet, was represented as having the head of a cat. Shasti, a Hindu goddess, rides a cat. In Norse mythology, the Scandinavian goddess Freyja traversed the skies in a chariot drawn by cats and directed white cats to carry out her orders on earth. She must have been quite powerful and supremely blessed to get cats to agree to all that.

Cats have long been associated with fertility through these mythological goddesses. This fertility link is also expressed in later folklore, superstition, and legend: it has been said that if a queen or tom house cat sneezes near a bride on her wedding morning, the bride will be fertile and happy in her conjugal bed. If the cat sneezes more than once, the bride will give birth to a like number of children.

In today's world, the rabbit seems to have grabbed the fertility mantle. The original logo for *Playboy* magazine was to be a cat, but somehow the bunny won out. I have it on good authority, however, that cats don't mind.

FIVE PHYSICAL BLESSINGS
THAT CATS ENJOY

QUICKNESS: A domestic cat can run at a speed of nearly 31 miles per hour. Pretty swift when you consider that a Thoroughbred racehorse clocks in about 35 to 38 miles per hour.

HEARING: Cats can rotate their ears independently by 180 degrees. They have thirty muscles in each ear and use about twelve of them to manipulate their ear movements. The ear rotations help them pick up sounds with more sensitivity than humans, and even dogs.

A cat's eyes are windows, enabling us to see into another world.

—IRISH LEGEND

FLEXIBILITY: A cat's body contains more bones and vertebrae than you'll find in a human body. Cats don't have a collarbone, but this blesses them with flexibility, which allows them to squeeze through head-sized openings. Almost 10 percent of a cat's bones are in her tail, helping a cat maintain exceptional balance.

SMELL: Cats have about 70 million scent-sensing cells. Humans operate with between 2 million and 20 million.

SIGHT: With eyes that have a layer of extra cells to absorb light, cats can see with about $\frac{1}{6}$ of the light it takes a human to see.

The Housecat's Prayer

Let me roam
But not too far from home
And grant me bush gardens to spy from
Protect me from fleas
And those buzzing peach bees
Forgive me for calling dogs Dumb

Let there be sunshine to lay in
Some boxes to play in
Along with food to keep me fed
And during the night
After they turn out the light
A place to curl up on the bed.

Blessed with a Free Spirit

The road most traveled is not his way.
Try for control, and he'll still have his say!
A cat must do what a cat must do.
He's an independent thinker
And free spirit through and through.

To please himself only the cat purrs.

— IRISH PROVERB

PLAYFUL AS A KITTEN

The blessing from kittens is the blessing of youth. The blessing of youth allows us see the world as new and alive with endless possibilities. Whether a kitten flops down wherever she feels like it, wraps herself around a ball and kicks away, or makes a mad dash just for the sake of dashing, the blessing for humans in witnessing such kitten antics is to be reminded that it's okay to let go of self-conscious inhibitions and that some playtime is every bit as important as work time.

When everything is going badly, it takes a kittenlike innocence to be hopeful and believe that things will turn out for the best. This positive hope gets you through seemingly hopeless times and stops any hole you're in from getting deeper. Hope is the residue of a playful outlook. So it's important to "lighten up" in the face of trials and fears. No fear can hold power over you if you have the playfulness to laugh at it; a daily lesson we are blessed to have our cats show us.

The Blessings of Understatement

A cat is never vulgar
She acts with Restraint and Grace
never forcing herself upon you
nor intruding upon your space.

While others might Demand,
or force their views on you
A cat is pleasant and accepting:
Signaling her take on things
with a demure and simple mew!

CATS IN THE GARDEN—
A MIXED BLESSING?

Humans aren't the only ones with an appreciation for greenery and flowers. Cats find "the jungle" of bushes, flowers, trees, and plants an evolutionary reminder of their hunting and stalking instincts, and of their kinship with nature. Cats, to the dismay of human gardeners, also find flower gardens to be great places for digging—and wonderful substitutes for litter boxes!

If the queen of your floral estate likes to use the garden as her literal "dumping ground," you can dissuade her. A litter box or sandbox on the garden perimeter often makes a good distraction—after all, familiarity breeds attempt. If she's still inclined to do her duty amongst the weeds and blooms, keep your garden beds moist with mulch. Cats don't like digging in damp substances. Also, marigolds and chamomile give off a scent that cats dislike. Spreading these plants throughout a garden can make "the regal one" think twice about digging and "doing" elsewhere.

A cat is a lion in a jungle of small bushes.

—FOLKSAYING FROM INDIA

Garden Patrol

The stealthy kitten at the tree
watches falling leaves intently.

To her, each fluttering parachute
appears a bird, a bug, or creature mute.

A crouch! A leap!
She meets halfway
the floating prize
the oncoming prey.

It's caught! It's conquered!
It won't get away!
A kitten triumphant, ruling the day.

The capture means the mystery's gone
But Look! Flower petals!
And she moves on.

THE GIFT OF GRACEFULNESS

Cats are blessed with elegance and grace, with dignity and presence. A cat's walk is a symphony of beautifully integrated movements that follow a silent harmonic rhythm flowing evenly over a terrain. If cats were musical instruments, they would be woodwinds playing soft haunting melodies, half sound, half gentle breeze. Even in repose, a cat's grace shows. Rather than sprawling out in awkward angles, a cat curls himself into a sensual cloud, blending into the couch, corner, or carpet he lies upon. Only a cat could make an old tattered pillow look pretty.

The Twenty-Third Cat Psalm

The world is my playground, please provide what I want.
Whether in verdant pastures or atop cushy beds
alloweth me repose.
Though I leaveth behind cat hair, a "gift" of mouse or bird,
or an occasional hairball, be pleased to honor me
and bid me come forth
by treats and toys and some tuna.
Even though I walk the dark valley of a finicky eater,
spread my foods before me.
For you know that only goodness, grace, and cuteness
follow me all the days of my life
And we shall dwell together in the house
I think of as mine.

BRIGHT-EYED AND
BUSHY-TAILED BLESSINGS

While no cat has (as yet) performed life-saving surgery, headed the Mayo Clinic, or created the definitive "super pill" for a happy and healthful life, numerous human studies on the effect of pets in our lives show that our furry friends bless us with physical and mental wellness in very special ways. Cats are bright-eyed and bushy-tailed and can help us become the same way.

In today's world, stress is a major culprit in breaking down our immune system and adding fuel to all kinds of physical maladies. Living furry animals, such as cats, offer a therapeutic blessing: stress reduction. Research has shown that stroking a cat can actually reduce our blood pressure (provided that the cat is not a 600-pound jungle cat looking at us as if we were lunch).

A study reported by the San Francisco Society for the Prevention of Cruelty to Animals found that people who had adopted cats or dogs reported fewer headaches, bouts of fever and indigestion, and cases of insomnia when compared to people who remained petless.

There are two means of refuge from the miseries of life: music and cats.

—ALBERT SCHWEITZER

The Medical Journal of Australia cited studies from the Baker Medical Research Institute in Melbourne, Australia, that found pet owners showed significantly lower systolic blood pressure and plasma triglycerides than petless people and displayed lower levels of recognized risk factors for cardiovascular disease.

Our own National Institute of Health (NIH), under a NIH Technology Assessment Statement titled "The Health Benefits of Pets," recognized that since relaxation, meditation, and stress management are bona fide preventative therapies for reducing blood pressure, it seemed reasonable that pets could provide a psychosocial stability for their owners and a measure of protection from heart disease. Many independent studies have indicated that having a pet increases a person's survival rate following a hospital stay for heart problems, while an Australian study titled, "The National People and Pets Survey," found that pet owners made fewer doctor visits and took fewer medications than people without pets.

It also appears that pet people recover more quickly from illness and surgery, and are better able to deal with stressful situations. And, in the case of Acquired Immune Deficiency Syndrome (AIDS), those patients who have a pet companion exhibit less depression and show reduced stress over the illness. Four-legged companions are a major source of support and help increase an AIDS-sufferer's ability to cope.

Cats may also be therapists and psychologists in disguise. What they can give is a healthy sense of optimism, be a hedge against loneliness and depression, and help break down barriers that might cause us to become isolated from others. Cats touch our lives and remind us of the blessings derived from interacting with others. No one can be a stone-cold hermit after having a kitten cuddle up in his lap. Cats listen without judging and love us unconditionally. And love is a pretty powerful prescription for whatever might ail us.

To heal a sty on an eyelid, rub it with the tail of a black cat.

—BRITISH AND AMERICAN FOLK REMEDY

A Confident Cat Came Calling

A cat came a-calling as I lie in my bed
feeling forlorn and somewhat half-dead.
An ache in the spirit; a pain in the heart,
my troubles overwhelmed me.
Where do I start?

Cats are designated friends.

—NORMAN CORWIN

Yet, sat the cat, having none of it,
"It's not so bad;
just see it through.
You can make it; I'm telling you!

"Start by taking a lesson from me:
size up the situation and see it realistically.
Then take a little action instead of worry and crying.
Keep going! Pounce ahead!
It's not in the crying, but in trying!"

I must admit that cat made sense:
Cut out the worry; get down off the fence.
For we all have the power to save our own day
when we're blessed with cat confidence
that won't be turned away.

*The cat
laps moonbeams
in the bowl of water,
thinking them to be milk.*

—HINDU PROVERB

TEN TINY BLESSINGS CATS GIVE

1. Cats cuddle.

2. Cats give us kittens.

3. Cats give our laps something to hold.

4. Cats lead us to meet other "cat people."

5. Cats teach us to ignore our mistakes and carry on.

6. Cats remind us that there are some things right in the world.

7. Cats decorate a windowsill like nothing else can.

8. Cats show us that it's okay to act spontaneously and go nuts for no plausible reason.

9. Cats ignore us and take us down a peg or two when we think we're totally in control.

10. Cats show us that sometimes the best way to come up with a solution is to sleep on the problem.

For there is nothing sweeter than his peace when at rest. For there is nothing brisker than his life when in motion.

—CHRISTOPHER SMART

THE CAT: BRINGING BLESSINGS IN ANY LANGUAGE

A rose, by any other name, is supposed to smell sweet; what then of cats?

Does the *gato* of Spain and Mexico ignore your calling the same way the *gatto* of Italy does? Does a Ukrainian *kotuk* have the same style and grace as a French *chat*? Will the *popoki* in Hawaii lie in the sun with the same luxuriant sprawl as the *neko* in Japan, the *katsi* in Africa, or the *kucing* in Indonesia?

Perhaps only the *kottur* of Iceland and the *cait* of Ireland will say for sure unless, of course a Korean *ko-yang-i's* got their tongue.

WHAT I'M SAYING IS .

Blessings from cats are benedictions even to the world of music. Besides the songs extolling a cat's actions and mischief in children's music, cats have inspired composers from classical works from the avant-garde to the Broadway stage.

Cat lover and composer Domenico Scarlatti, so the story goes, composed *The Cat Fugue* (Sonata no. 30, in G-minor) from the six random notes his cat struck while walking across the keys of his harpsichord! The full composition is quite lively but in places captures the elegant sense of importance cats seem to pride themselves in. The cat's six notes, an unusual mix of high, middle, and low notes, reoccur throughout the piece as if the cat is again waking the keys.

A similar story surrounds Chopin's "The Cat Waltz" (op. 34/3). The great composer integrated into the work the tones his cat "played" while running across the piano keys as composed a waltz in F-Major! Chopin himself didn't title his pieces, but the nickname for this particular waltz has stood the test of time; and cats continue to waltz to it.

Cats are written and sung about in many other songs, plays, poems, and operas. Among Igor Stravinsky's Russian folk pieces, you'll find his Cat's Cradle Songs. In 1966, Stravinsky composed *The Owl and the Pussycat* based upon a favorite poem written by

Edward Lear. Prokofiev musically denoted the cat in *Peter and the Wolf* through the use of woodwinds played softly and sensually, while Rossini tuned into the playfulness of cats in his *Duetto Buffo dei due Gatti* (A Comic Duet for Two Cats), and Ravel turned to cat love in his opera, *L'Enfant et les Sortileges* (The Child and the Magic Spells), as two cats sang a love duet in feline language.

For his ballet *The Sleeping Beauty*, Tschaikovsky composed "The White Cat Waltz" for a dance based upon feline movements. It takes place between Puss-in-Boots and White Cat.

To be totally immersed in the blessings of cat song and cat dance takes a performance of Andrew Lloyd Weber's musical extravaganza, *Cats*. Since catwalking onto the landscape of the London stage in 1981, then onto the West End and Broadway, the play has won numerous awards worldwide, along with appreciation from actual cats.

Yes, cats have played a big part in the world of symphonic ballet and dance. They even have a movement named after them, the *pas de chat;* a graceful but difficult ballet jump in which the feet are lofted, separately, to the level of the opposite knee. A dancer needs the agility of a cat, hence the term.

Of course, on the modern hip-and-cool musical scene, who can top a jazz cat? Jazzman Zez Confrey set the tone for an era of jazz musicians with his lively and playful composition "Kitten on the Keys" in which he painted a musical scene of a cat running across a piano keyboard. Combining old ragtime licks with the newer jazz impressionism, and overtones of improvisational jazz, Confrey created a style of "novelty piano" that was all the rage in the 1920s. His inspiration? A blessedly mischievous cat who awakened him one night by promenading back and forth across the keyboard of an old-fashioned upright piano! An even earlier jazz ditty, "The Black Cat Rag," helped establish Ethel B. Smith as a composer and song writer in 1905. Smith was one of America's first female composers and collaborated with Frank Wooster on her breakthrough piece.

A MUSICAL BLESSING FOR CATS?

Musician, composer, and producer Jim Romeo records music created especially for cats at Romeo Music International in Framingham, Massachusetts.

"The Music for Cats and Kittens" is an audio CD, which is marketed worldwide and on the Internet (www.romeomusic.com/funforcats/). Romeo found that cats are great listeners! He conducted his own testing to discover the types of sounds cats and kittens respond to positively: the sounds of bells and high-pitched tones in general, and the "plucked" notes of harps and the like. Very low tones are intriguing, while musical starts and stops seem to enhance a cat's playtime!

With all this in mind, Romeo Music produces sumptuous cat-friendly versions of musical compositions ranging from Scarlatti and Haydn to Chopin, Brahms, and Bach. Lightheartedly, Vivaldi's "Spring," contains some soft birdcalls woven within it that cats find especially interesting. Musical cat blessings, it seems, can work in many ways!

Dancing to Their Own Music

Cats will dance anywhere
A limbo under the table
A pirouette with a leg of the chair.

They'll waltz 'round your ankles
but never step on your toes.
Cats samba and rumba with each other.
They can tango nose to nose.

The rhythm that they dance to
comes from the music they feel inside.
We can learn much from cats dancing:
Be joyous, free, and open;
     you really have nothing to hide.

What is it that cats see when they go into their nearly "catatonic" stares into space? Simply put, a cat's eyesight is extraordinarily sharp, able to detect very slight movements occurring a short distance away. Physically put, since their eyes are set far forward on the face, cats have exceptional binocular vision allowing them to pinpoint an object or prey while leaving the rest of their visual field in a blur. Cats can focus pretty sharply on things just beyond their immediate reach. However, they can't focus as well on nearby objects. But beyond the physicality and explainable mechanics of a cat's sight, what is it that cats see with "the stare?" Is there a sixth sense alerting cats to things that we humans neither see nor hear?

It makes me stop and wonder
Every time I see
A cat seeing something
That I never see.

The British have a proverb that states, "The cat sees through shut lids." And indeed, cats seem to see not only through closed eyes but also into dimensions we humans can't see.

A nineteenth century poet and author Theophile Gautier said, "Who can believe that there is no soul behind those luminous eyes!" Is there a psychic or spiritual intuition that allows cats to view a place beyond our physical-material realm? We can only guess. But if angels and guardian spirits are nearby, and if there's more to our lives than just the physical realities we see, then a heightened sensitivity might allow the spirits to come into view, or at least be felt in some way. Cats operate nonjudgmentally, instinctively, and perceptually, so they can tune in to things we humans have a hard time perceiving (our "antennas" pick up a lot of static in our oh-so-busy daily lives). And maybe there's more out there than just what meets the human eye. Are cats blessed with "the stare" that allows them to see beyond a limited vision? Are they special little beings straddling two worlds immersed in the same physical space? It's fun to think so. It may even be true. Cats, at this point, aren't telling.

So take a little time out of the chaos and commotion to simply watch a cat watching something (nothing?) with that alert, unblinking stare. Maybe you'll feel an angel nearby.

When they are among us, cats are angels.

—GEORGE SAND

An Independent Contractor

Give an order to a cat?
Don't make me laugh!
I tried that once, just to see.

He pondered a minute
Felt nothing was in it
Then said he'd get back to me!

The Gift Giver

On Monday it was a field mouse
alive
let loose
and scurrying through the house.

On Tuesday it was a baby bird
playing dead
pried away
and returned to its mother without a word.

Wednesday brought a grasshopper.
How he caught it I'll never know.
Thursday was a bone of some kind
That one he wouldn't let go.

Friday he stayed out all night.
Saturday he hunted flies, but was bested.
Then came Sunday, and the hunt was over
Thank God, that day he rested.

For when he takes his prey he plays with it to give it chance. For one mouse in seven escapes by his dallying . . .

—CHRISTOPHER SMART ON HIS CAT JEOFFREY FROM *JUBILATE AGNO*

The Universal Gift

There is one little "blessing"
that cats might need not send
But if you live with cats
you'll get it
and receive it without end.

You'll find it floating everywhere.
You'll wear it wherever you go.
Your closet, couch, and carpet
are "blessed"
and, oh, how it will show.

Even the corners of the curtains
will tell who's just been there.
It's the feline form of decorating
cat hair everywhere!

Anthropologist Margaret Mead was quoted as saying, "One of the oldest human needs is having someone to wonder where you are when you don't come home at night." Humans have a basic instinct to be connected, to feel validated as something worthwhile to a source outside themselves. One of the great blessings pets bring us is an unconditional, nonjudgmental presence that responds and communicates with us.

Cats bless us as "security blankets" at night, cuddled up nearby. They make trustworthy confidants who won't "spill the beans" about us. And, in those melancholy moments that we hide from others, there is a soft reassurance and a tactile comfort in holding and petting a cat.

Cats seem to react to our grief and pain, reading those disturbing vibes we're sending out and coming to us with understanding and a helping paw. I was laid out flat on the floor of my living room with a back injury some years ago. My bed was too high to tackle, but I could crawl on my stomach from the floor onto a bed of some makeshift pillows. Harold, my stalwart white cat companion at the time, surveyed the situation, came up to me, nose-to-nose, took notice of my limited movements and grimaces of pain, and "moved in" exactly within petting distance, keeping guard and offering sympathy over the month I was out of commission. We watched the baseball playoffs and World Series together, both of us lying on our stomachs.

Cats also bless us with the warmth of recognition and give us a sense of connection. It makes a difference in the world that we're alive and that we're there. This blessing of companionship can ward off loneliness, work as a safeguard from depression, and spur us to break down barriers that isolate us from human contact—having one friend leads to developing others. Pets allow us to experience bonding with another living entity and also provide us with the opportunity for simple play and relaxation.

It is ironic that in today's overcrowded urban lifestyles, we can still feel isolated, lonely, and vulnerable. Medical studies show that people who feel isolated and deprived of human contact and interaction experience a lower sense of well-being, health, self-worth, and joy than those who feel "connected." Cats help connect us to the whole spectrum of life. French poet, filmmaker, and cat lover Jean Cocteau feels that, in a home, cats "become its visible soul."

As soul mates, loves, nurses, confidants, and official family members, cats bless us with a special kind of companionship.

GOOD GROOMING SHOULD NOT BE IGNORED AS A BLESSING!

Cats are amazing self-grooming systems. In fact after sleeping, grooming and preening take up most of a cat's time— more than one-third of their waking hours! Fastidiousness, thy name is feline!

A cat seems to always be looking to put his best paw forward and present an assured, confident appearance. There is a blessing for humans in this. Psychologically speaking, your dress and appearance communicate to the world at large how you feel about yourself and how you expect to be treated; it's also a way to tell yourself that you've got it all together. Your image of yourself affects who you are—if you see yourself as a competent, attractive, and self-assured person, you'll become one. A consistent diet of "letting yourself go" and sloppiness brings you mentally down to that level.

Cats bless you with the idea of being and looking your best for the world and for yourself. This can make a big difference in how you feel about yourself and your world. Feeling on top of things, you exude an air of confidence and competency that can open doors to both people and success. It's a subtle blessing that can work wonders in strengthening yourself and giving you a sense of your own worth.

If a cat washes his face, there will be visitors.

—FOLKLORE

So Says the Siamese

My meticulous cleaning
is more than vanity and preening
It's what I am all about

Presenting a face
with each hair neatly in place
gives you a lot more clout.

I have breeding and class
walk with elegance and sass
There's a confidence and cool air

So when I fidget and fuss
regard it a plus
I'm dressed to go anywhere!

Siamese cats have crossed eyes because they spent so much time staring at the golden goblet of Buddha.

—A LEGEND OF THE SIAMESE CAT
FROM THAILAND

SIX CATS BRINGING BLESSINGS OF LAUGHTER AND MIRTH

THE CAT IN THE HAT: This whimsical cat was born out of a list of 400 words given to Dr. Seuss (Theodor Seuss Geisel) by his publisher who wanted the writer to concoct a children's story of about 250 words from the list. The cat became a hit and gave school-aged children a new interest in reading.

MORRIS THE CAT: The haughty and finicky orange-colored star of cat food commercials on television set the benchmark for comic aloofness.

THE CHESHIRE CAT: Lewis Carroll's magical Cheshire left only his broad grin behind as he slowly disappeared in the book *Alice's Adventures in Wonderland.*

FELIX THE CAT: This mischievous cat with his "bag of tricks" has been pulling comic antics in cartoon strips, comic books, and movies since 1919.

SYLVESTER: The slapstick fall guy in hundreds of Warner Bros. cartoons, Sylvester still has not bested his all-consuming interest, Tweety. "Sufferin' succotash!"

GARFIELD: A bug-eyed sarcastic trickster, Garfield leaves no doubt that he is in charge of the human world he surveys.

A Blessed Imagination

The Tennis Ball rolling away
is Captured
Clawed
and Kicked as prey

A Falling Paper
appears a gull in flight
Crouch,
and Watch
then Pounce in delight

Spaghetti strands of Dangling String,
an adversarial air force taken wing
Reach and Bat
Flick and Fling
then on to the next imaginary thing . . .

To be in the company of cats is a study in independence. Cats go their own singular way.

Cats evolved from highly territorial ancestors. They are not the "pack" animals that dogs are and, thus, are not driven to please or follow the leader, or to take on a prescribed role as part of a group. Cats don't try to win favor or status but rather set up their own ways of dealing with their surroundings, and they survive by following an individual instinct.

Cats star in their own lives and won't play a character role in somebody else's. The solitary cat answers to himself alone and jumps to no group's social command. Even the domesticated house cat maintains his link to his wild side. If allowed to go outside, a cat goes alone without looking back for a "pack mate" (owner) like a dog generally does.

A cat does not have a desire for a leash, a walk in the park with an owner, or a game of Frisbee. A cat has some business of his own to tend to and will catch up with his person later when he determines it's time to come home. A cat's home is his base; a dog's home is his world.

Cats bless us with a sense of individuality. It's a lesson in following our own instincts, being happy with who we are, and expressing the

KEEP OUT

individuality that makes us, well, us! As humans, we're tied to many conventions, but for life to be fully lived, we've got to test the rules and sometimes modify them. By cats' individuality and independence, they are telling us it's okay to follow our curiosity, to believe in ourselves, and trust our own inner voice.

Cats are the entrepreneurs, while dogs are the middle-managers of the world. Dogs are most comfortable following the rules, while cats seem bent on breaking them. Cats are the Robin Hoods and Lone Rangers of life, while dogs are more inclined to be part of The Magnificent Seven. There's no "best" in either way, but in a world that's becoming less and less differentiated the bigger and bigger it gets, more individuality and independent ideas sure couldn't hurt.

BLESSED WITH LUCK?

The Maneki Neko ("the beckoning cat") is a good-luck cat figurine in Japan.

Displays of this traditional Japanese good-luck charm welcome people to Kansai International Airport in Osaka. There, three large versions carry greetings to visitors in seven languages.

Shopkeepers in Japan often display Maneki Neko at the entrances and throughout their stores as a blessing for good business. A Maneki Neko raising its left paw is inviting people to come to it; a raised right paw is said to bring happiness and money. And take note of their various colors: white ones bring joy; black keeps evil spirits away; gold attracts money; and red keeps plague from your door (hopefully throughout your nine lives).

Kiss a black cat,
an' twill make ye fat;
Kiss a white cat,
an' twill make ye lean.

—ENGLISH FOLKLORE

MANEKI-NEKO

In Britain, tortoiseshell cats are said to bring luck to their owners. In Russia, blue cats bring luck.

—FOLK LEGENDS

The Cat Person's Multiplication Table

One cat needs a friend
 so then you have two
Somehow a third comes along
and what can you do?

The fourth was so sad-eyed
and needed a home
But when you picked her up
her sister came along.

The neighbor moved out
And guess what—left the cat!
How can people abandon
a sweetheart like that!!

The kind elderly lady
down the block passed away
She left you her darling
Now he has to stay.

People always find you
bringing sad stories and strays
You say "No, I can't!"
But in the end, the cat stays.

You're a bona fide Cat Person
A huge heart and veterinary bill
You swear you're getting rid of them all!
(But, of course, you never will.)

THE BLESSINGS OF THE HERE AND NOW

Cats appear to have a Buddhist-like attitude toward life and their place in it. Beyond the idea of stopping to smell the roses (or catnip plants), cats sit and savor the present—whatever garden they're in—and live in the moment. Cats fall into harmony with their surroundings, whether it's a plush cushion or a feral cat trap, and find a peace that's a lesson and blessing for all of us.